W9-BHS-810

BIOMIMICRY

AWESOME INNOVATIONS
INSPIRED BY
BIRDS

Jim Corrigan

Mitchell Lane

PUBLISHERS

mitchelllane.com

2001 SW 31st Avenue
Hallandale, FL 33009

First Edition, 2021.
Author: Jim Corrigan
Designer: Ed Morgan
Editor: Sharon F. Doorasamy

Series: Biomimicry
Title: Awesome Innovations Inspired by Birds / by Jim Corrigan

Hallandale, FL : Mitchell Lane Publishers, [2021]

Library bound ISBN: 978-1-68020-603-6
eBook ISBN: 978-1-68020-604-3

PHOTO CREDITS: cover: Shutterstock, p. 6 freepik.com, p. 7 Nareeta Martin unsplash.com, p. 9 public domain, pp. 10-11 freepik.com, p. 13 Sydney Rae unsplash.com, p. 14 Flickr User Rui Ornelas CC-BY-SA-2.0, p. 15 Mike Peel CC-BY-SA-4.0, pp. 16-17 Will Bolding unsplash.com, pp. 18-19 CEphoto, Uwe Aranas / CC-BY-SA-3.0, p. 21 Getty Images, p. 22 Public Domain, p. 23 Dharmit Shah unsplash.com, p. 25 freepik.com, p. 26 Bill Pennell unsplash.com, p. 27 Peripitus CC-BY-SA-3.0-migrated

Contents

Master of the Sky

In July 2019, a small plane crept down a runway in Filton, England. The jet had no passengers. It was an experiment.

Engineers from a company called Airbus watched it gain speed. They had named their test plane *AlbatrossOne*. With it, they hoped to uncover the secrets of nature's greatest glider.

The albatross is a majestic sea bird and master of the sky. Its unique wings can go more than 70 miles (113 kilometers) without flapping. The engineers admired the albatross's gliding ability. They gave their test plane similar wings.

AlbatrossOne left the runway and soared high into the air. Its wingtips flapped and fluttered. The wings looked strange, but they worked. Gusty winds posed no problem. *AlbatrossOne* used the gusts for extra lift. The little jet glided almost as gracefully as the bird it copied.

The Airbus engineers smiled and hugged. Their first experiment had succeeded. Many more tests would come, but they were off to a good start. Thanks to the albatross, tomorrow's planes might fly farther and use less fuel.

People at companies like Airbus hunt for new ideas. They never stop trying to improve their product or service. When someone finds a better way to do something, it's called **innovation**.

The race to innovate never ends. A hundred years ago, radio was the newest way to communicate. Today, we have the Internet and smartphones. Future innovators will find even better ways to stay connected.

chapter one

Nature's Innovations

We are not the only species to innovate. Life first appeared on Earth more than 3.5 billion years ago. Since then, countless species have found clever ways to survive. The gecko developed sticky feet to climb steep rocks and cling under leaves. Without this innovation, the gecko might have gone extinct.

Humans often look to nature for great ideas. Gecko feet have inspired climbing tools and sticky tape. In space, astronauts use "gecko gripper" pads to hold objects in place. Borrowing ideas from nature is called **biomimicry**. (*Bio* means "life" and *mimic* means "to copy.") Today's innovators use biomimicry to solve problems in our complex world.

Gecko feet have inspired climbing tools and sticky tape.

Birds have been flitting around this planet for more than 150 million years. Most scientists consider them living dinosaurs. They survived the asteroid impact that killed off the other dinosaurs.

During their long history, birds have made some remarkable innovations. The albatross teaches us about gliding, but many other species offer valuable lessons.

FUN FACT

The albatross glides so well that scientists suspect it can sleep in midair. Naps must come in handy when you circle the globe in just 46 days!

Spreading Our Wings

Ancient humans envied birds. A Greek myth told of Icarus, who learned to fly with wings of wax and feathers. When Icarus flew too close to the sun, his waxy wings melted. He plunged to the sea and drowned.

The myth is a warning about being too confident, yet it tells us something else. Ancient people wanted to mimic birds, but they had no idea how to do it.

Much later, around the year 1505, the famous innovator Leonardo da Vinci studied birds. He wrote a book about their methods of flight. His book included sketches for flying machines. Leonardo da Vinci never flew, but he did inspire others to carry on his work.

The dream of flight finally became real in 1903. On a gray December day, Orville and Wilbur Wright stood on a windswept beach. They had spent years observing birds and designing airplanes. Orville climbed onto the flimsy *Wright Flyer* and coaxed its engine to life. His little plane scuttled across the sand. At last, it lifted into the air.

Orville flew for just 12 seconds and climbed only 10 feet (3 meters) high. Still, for the first time, the seagulls had company.

Wilbur Wright ran beside the plane to help balance it. In this photo, he has just let go of the right wing.

chapter two

Old Idea, New Name

Leonardo da Vinci and the Wright brothers had used biomimicry, but they didn't know it. The word had not yet been invented. A science writer named Janine Benyus coined the term in 1997. She wrote a book entitled *Biomimicry: Innovation Inspired by Nature*.

Janine Benyus wrote her book as an urgent reminder. She worried that we had forgotten nature's genius. The modern world relied on faceless companies and unfeeling computers. Engineers worked in sterile labs. Innovators had become **isolated** from nature. As a result, Benyus said, we no longer looked to plants and animals for great ideas.

She pointed to a big difference between humans and nature. People create a lot of garbage. The world makes 3.5 million tons of plastic and other solid waste every single day.

Nature wastes nothing. When a tree dies, termites break it down into fresh soil for new plants. The more we mimic nature, the less garbage we will produce.

Fortunately, the world is catching on. Biomimicry now yields a wealth of new ideas and solutions. Many of those discoveries are coming from the realm of birds.

Friends of a Feather

The next time you see a duck floating on a pond, pay attention. You are looking at a survival expert. Ducks can be found on every continent except Antarctica.

Baby ducks, or ducklings, are ready to leave home after just two months. They feel comfortable on land, in the air, or on water. Their webbed feet can paddle in the most frigid pond without freezing.

A thick layer of fluff called "down" keeps a duck's body warm. Thin, rigid feathers enable it to fly. Like most birds, a duck **preens** itself. Each feather gets waxed to keep it waterproof and flight worthy. Ducks can teach us how to adapt to a changing environment.

Better Builders

Architects marvel at the nests of some birds. Hummingbirds, for example, can build a nest that expands as their babies grow.

The hummingbird first raids spider webs, taking the strong, stretchy silk. Next it adds tree bark and leaf strands. Finally, it covers the nest with lichens for **camouflage**. The hummingbird's hatchlings grow up in a safe and spacious home.

An African bird named the sociable weaver erects the largest nest in the world. It is basically an apartment building, housing more than 200 sociable weavers. The gigantic nest, which looks like a haystack, can fill an entire tree. Every resident helps with its upkeep.

Sociable weavers are amazing architects. They use twigs, grasses, fur, cotton, fluff, and soft plant materials to build their nests. Some of these nest "hotels" have remained occupied for more than 100 years.

Sociable weaver nests do an amazing job of staying cool in summer and warm in winter.

Brilliant Birds

People use the word "birdbrain" as an insult, but the joke is on them. Studies have shown some species are extremely clever.

African gray parrots can learn roughly 1,000 words. They know shapes and colors. In Tokyo, an African gray named Yosuke escaped from his cage and got lost. Strangers brought him home after Yosuke repeated his owner's name and address.

Crows are very **observant**. They recognize human faces and remember if a person was kind or mean to them. If a crow sees a mean person coming, it will call out a warning to other crows.

Crows have brains the size of an average human thumb, but research shows they are as clever as a seven-year-old child.

The crow's larger cousin, the raven, is a skilled problem-solver. In one experiment, scientists locked food inside a box that could only be opened with a special tool. They showed a group of ravens how to use the tool. The ravens learned to unlock the box and get their treat.

The scientists returned many times with the same box. They offered the ravens a variety of tools. Almost every time, the ravens chose the correct tool to open the box. Ravens and other smart species are helping us unravel mysteries of the brain.

China's Beijing National Stadium is nicknamed the Bird's Nest. A unique steel frame surrounds the stadium but does not touch it. Architects designed the Bird's Nest to last 100 years. Built for the 2008 Summer Olympics Games in Beijing, the Nest will host the 2022 Winter Olympic and Paralympic Games.

Biomimicry in Action

The West Japan Railway Company had a problem. Its high-speed trains, or bullet trains, were too noisy. They moved so fast that they created a loud shock wave. Their boom rattled windows and jolted people from their beds.

The railway hired a team of engineers, led by a man named Eiji Nakatsu. He happened to be a bird watcher. Nakatsu believed birds could help him design a quieter train. He looked to species known for being silent and **streamlined**.

The owl, for example, is a quiet hunter. Rats and mice never hear it coming. An owl's feathers have tiny notches that break up the noise of flowing air. Nakatsu's team gave their train notches like owl feathers.

Next they looked at penguin bellies. The Adelie penguin uses its smooth belly to slide across the ice. In water, the streamlined penguin can virtually fly. The team shaped part of the train like an Adelie's belly.

Their best innovation came from a bird called the kingfisher. When a kingfisher spots a fish, it dives straight down into the water. The kingfisher then grabs its prey before launching itself back into the air. This spectacle happens in the blink of an eye.

Incredibly, the diving kingfisher barely makes a splash. Its beak and head have evolved to slice through the water. The team borrowed this shape for the nose of their train.

The bird-inspired bullet train worked better than expected. It traveled faster than previous trains and used less energy. Best of all, the shock wave was gone. Passengers had a smoother ride, and people living near the train tracks could sleep.

The Japanese bullet trains are quiet and fast.

chapter four

Ostrich Bot

Let's face it, ostriches look silly. These huge, flightless birds strut around on gangly legs. They have a long, bare neck that juts up from a shaggy body. No ostrich will ever win a beauty contest.

Engineers at the company Boston Dynamics disagree. They admire the world's largest living bird. In 2019, they unveiled a robot that looks like an ostrich. It can work in a warehouse, moving and stacking boxes.

The first version of the warehouse robot looked more like a human. It had arms and stood upright. The ostrich bot is different. It has a long neck and suction cups on its head for picking up heavy boxes.

When an ostrich bot bends for a box, its rear end swings up in the air. The bot might look a bit silly, just like the bird, but it does a great job. Someday, ostrich bots may work in warehouses around the world.

The humanoid robot Atlas (pictured here) was created by Boston Dynamics to negotiate rough outdoor terrain. Atlas stands 6 feet 2 inches tall and weighs 330 pounds.

FUN FACT

Ostriches can run 45 miles (70 kilometers) per hour, and their kick can kill a lion. In the future, robots with ostrich-style legs might rescue people from disaster areas.

Bird-Based Future

Birds still give us flying lessons and likely will do so long into the future. Imagine a drone as swift and nimble as a bird.

Today's drones still need a flat spot to land. Researchers at Yale University hope to change that. They are working on a drone with birdlike feet. It will be able to perch on a tree branch, or even hang upside down. Perching drones could deliver cargo to people living in jungles or steep mountains.

Brain Savers

Football is America's most popular sport, but doctors worry about football players. Hard hits often lead to brain injury. Fortunately, a head-banging bird might be able to help.

Woodpeckers spend their days pounding on trees. They peck at the wood, looking for bugs to eat. A typical peck has 10 times more force than a football tackle. Yet, as far as we can tell, woodpeckers suffer no brain injury.

Today, many football players wear helmets and neck collars inspired by woodpeckers. But the story doesn't end there. Scientists are now looking at a **protein** in the brain called tau.

Players who suffer long-term brain injury have a buildup of tau. Too much tau is bad for the brain. It leads to diseases like Alzheimer's and Parkinson's. In 2018, a group of scientists checked woodpecker brains for tau. To their shock, the woodpeckers also had a tau buildup, just like the players.

chapter five

Woodpeckers have special bones in their skull that act like a seat-belt. The bones keep the brain comfortable and protect against concussions.

No one knows yet why woodpeckers can tolerate tau. If science solves this mystery, the benefits will go beyond football. People with deadly brain diseases might be saved.

Nature holds many amazing secrets for us to unlock. Biomimicry is the act of copying nature to solve human problems. Natural solutions do not harm the environment. With biomimicry, people in science and business are finding tomorrow's ideas today.

Professor Erich Jarvis of Rockefeller University studies the brains of songbirds. Male zebra finches learn complex songs, which they sing to attract females. Professor Jarvis believes songbirds like the zebra finch can shed light on human speech. Someday, his research might help people with speech disorders like stuttering.

What You Should Know

Birds are living dinosaurs. During their 150 million years on Earth, birds have evolved because they developed many clever survival tricks.

Humans tried for centuries to mimic birds in flight. The Wright brothers finally succeeded in 1903.

In addition to flight, birds have inspired innovation in train design, architecture, and medicine.

Birds such as parrots, crows, and ravens are intelligent. They can communicate, solve problems, and use tools.

The smart ideas that come from biomimicry have an extra benefit. They are safe for the environment.

A woodpecker's brain might hold the answers to human brain diseases such as Alzheimer's and Parkinson's.

Want to be an engineer?
Architect? Inventor?

1. Take math and science classes

2. Enroll in art and design classes

3. Attend STEM camps and programs

4. Visit nature preserves and parks to observe nature at work

5. Keep a journal or a blog of your observations

6. Enter science fairs and competitions

7. Check out books on biomimicry from your school and public library

8. Visit natural history museums and science centers

9. Check your community's calendar for talks by science and technology experts

10. Volunteer for citizen science events like bird counts, water sample collection, and weather reporting

Glossary

biomimicry
Borrowing ideas from nature

camouflage
To hide something by changing its appearance

innovation
To create or improve an object or method

isolated
Separated or set apart

observant
Alert; quick to notice details

preen
To trim or clean with the beak or tongue

protein
A substance found in all living animals and plant cells; it's made up of amino acids

streamlined
Shaped to offer the least resistance to flowing air or water

Online Resources

Visit the Conservationist for Kids webpage
www.dec.ny.gov/education/40248.html for more information about: Biomimicry, Green Chemistry, Green Schools, and Sustainability

Check out the Ask Nature website
www.asknature.org

Listen to Janine Benyus talk about biomimicry
www.ted.com/speakers/janine_benyus

Enjoy the podcast 30 Animals That Made Us Smarter
www.bbc.co.uk/programmes/w13xttw7

Search YouTube
for videos on biomimicry

Visit
www.uspto.gov/kids/Biomimicry.pdf

Learn to identify North American bird species
www.audubon.org/bird-guide

Further Reading

Nandi, Ishani, ed. *Everything You Need to Know About Birds*. DK Children, 2016.

Koontz, Robin. *Nature-Inspired Contraptions*. Rourke Educational Media, 2018.

Colby, Jennifer. *Woodpeckers to Helmets: Tech from Nature*. Cherry Lake Publishing, 2019.

Becker, Helaine, and Alex Ries. *Zoobots: Wild Robots Inspired by Real Animals*. Kids Can Press, 2014.

Index

About the Author

Jim Corrigan has been writing nonfiction for more than 20 years. He holds degrees from Penn State and Johns Hopkins. Jim became a fan of biomimicry while working on a book about airplanes. He currently lives near Philadelphia.